Human Body Systems

The Circulatory System

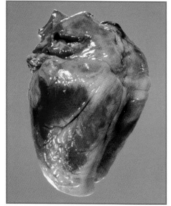

by Rebecca Olien

Consultant:
Marjorie Hogan, MD
Pediatrician
Hennepin County Medical Center
Minneapolis, Minnesota

Capstone press

Mankato, Minnesota

Bridgestone Books are published by Capstone Press,
151 Good Counsel Drive, P.O. Box 669, Mankato, Minnesota 56002.
www.capstonepress.com

Library of Congress Cataloging-in-Publication Data
Olien, Rebecca.
   The circulatory system / by Rebecca Olien.
      p. cm.—(Bridgestone books. Human body systems)
   Summary: "Learn about the job of the circulatory system, problems that may arise, and how to
keep the system healthy"—Provided by publisher.
   Includes bibliographical references and index.
   ISBN-13: 978-0-7368-5408-5 (hardcover)
   ISBN-10: 0-7368-5408-8 (hardcover)
      1. Cardiovascular system—Juvenile literature. I. Title. II. Bridgestone Books. Human body systems.
QP103.O45 2006
612.1—dc22   2005021145

Editorial Credits
Amber Bannerman, editor; Bobbi J. Dey, designer; Kelly Garvin, photo researcher/photo editor

Photo Credits
Capstone Press/Karon Dubke, cover (boy), 4
Corbis/Frans Lanting, 6; Images.com, 14; Michele Westmorland, 20; Richard T. Nowitz, 12
Getty Images Inc./Photodisc Green, cover (circulatory system)
Peter Arnold Inc./Alex Grey, 8
Visuals Unlimited/Biodisc, 18; Dr. Kessel & Dr. Kardon/Tissue & Organs, 16;
   Dr. Stanley Flegler, 10; SIU, 1

Table of Contents

Your Heartbeat

Thump thump. Thump thump. That is the sound of your heart beating. Your heart pumps blood to keep you alive. Blood travels to the top of your head and to the tips of your toes through the circulatory system.

The circulatory system is just one of your body's amazing systems. You can move because your systems work together. When you dance, run, and hop, you breathe harder, sweat, and get thirsty. Being active also gets your heart racing and your blood flowing.

◄ You can feel your pulse, or heartbeat, at your wrist.

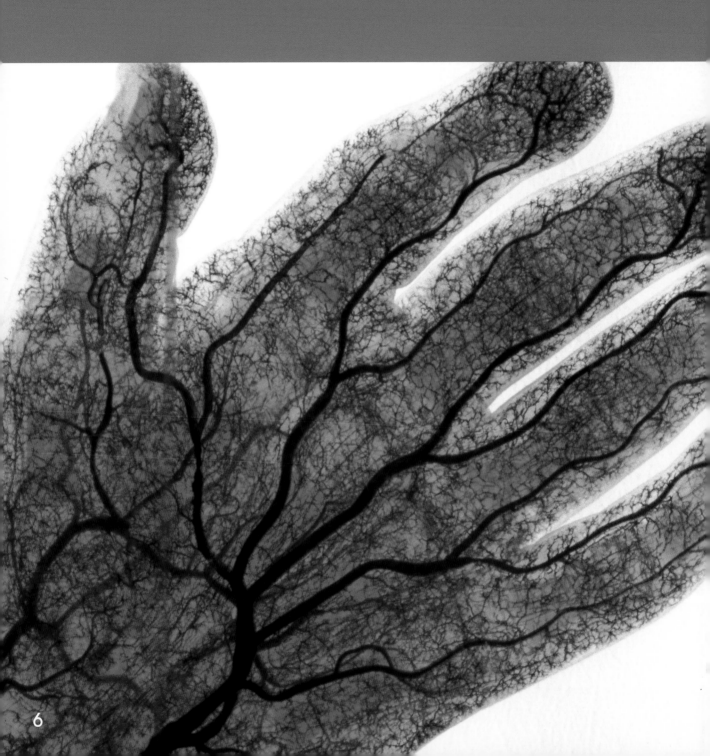

Blood and Waste

Blood must reach every part of the body to deliver needed oxygen to **cells**. Blood carries oxygen to cells through small tubes called **blood vessels**. Cells can't live without a constant supply of fresh blood.

While cells take in oxygen, they also get rid of waste. If waste never left your body, you'd get very sick. Blood collects cell waste and carries it to the lungs and the kidneys. From there, waste leaves the body.

◄ Blood vessels branch out to reach every part of the body.

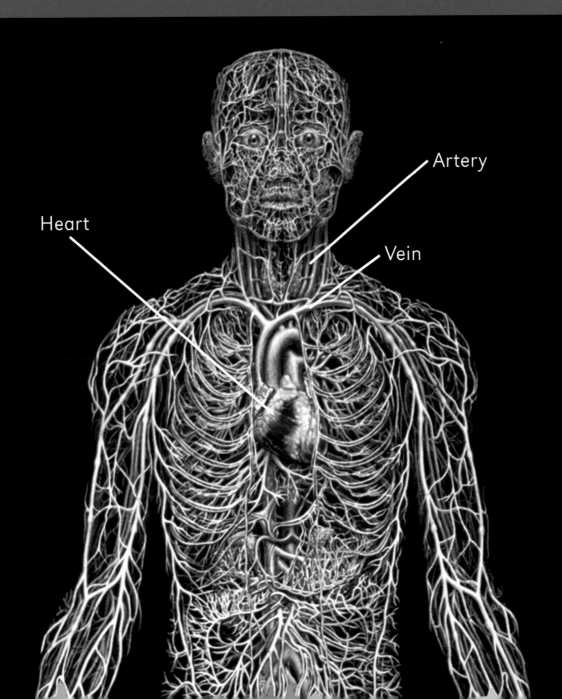

Artery

Vein

Heart

Parts of the Circulatory System

Your pumping heart and branching blood vessels work together to transport blood. Your heart is a muscle. It lies in the center of your chest, just under your breastbone.

Veins, **arteries**, and **capillaries** are types of blood vessels. They are found throughout the body. Veins bring blood to the heart, while arteries carry blood away from it. Capillaries connect to arteries and veins, and carry blood to even the smallest parts of the body.

◄ Red arteries take blood away from the heart, while blue veins bring it back.

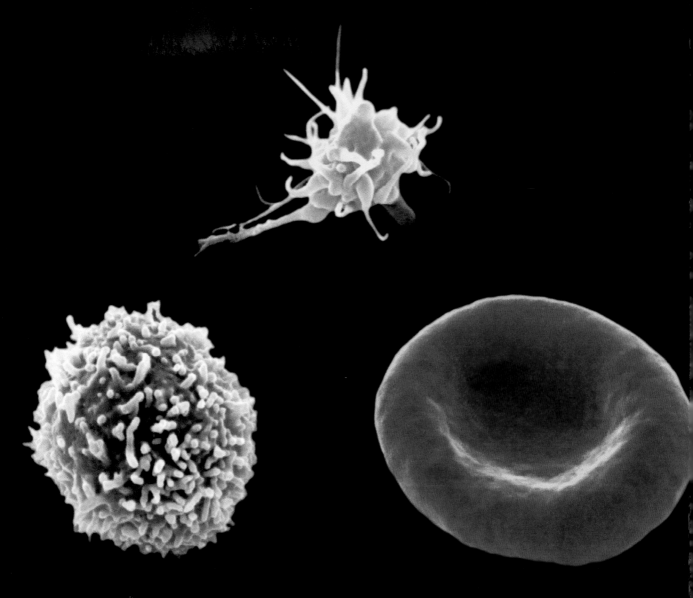

Parts of Blood

Have you ever wondered what your blood is made of? Water makes up most of it. Also floating around are red and white blood cells. Red blood cells contain **hemoglobin**. Hemoglobin carries oxygen and gives blood its red color. White blood cells help your body fight sicknesses.

Platelets are another part of blood. When you get a cut, platelets stop the bleeding. They clump together to plug a cut blood vessel.

◄ White blood cells (left), red blood cells (right), and platelets (top) are parts of blood.

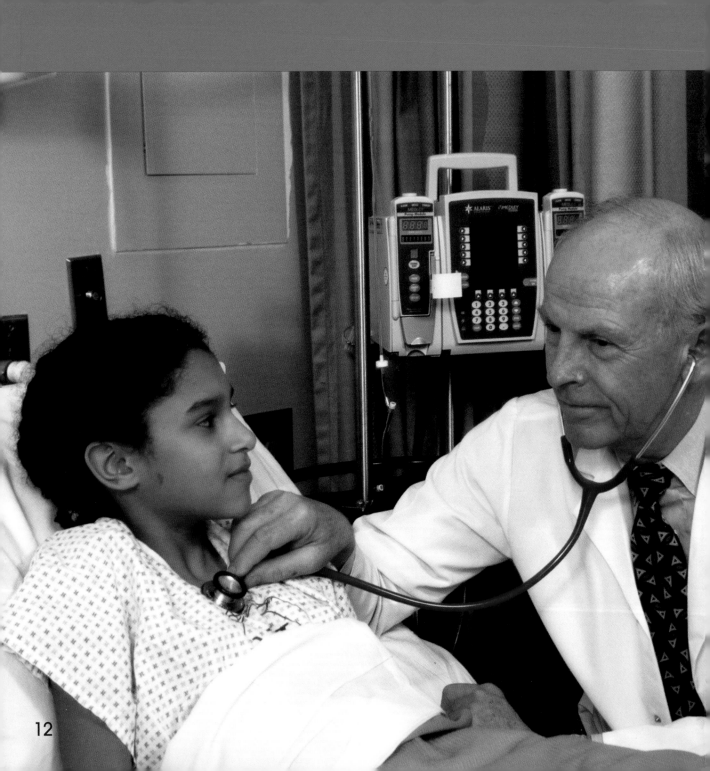

Your Amazing Heart

Your heart is about the size of your fist. This small muscle does a huge job. Your heart is the only muscle in your body that doesn't need rest. It works nonstop day and night without you even thinking about it.

Doctors listen to your thumping heartbeat to learn how your heart is working. During normal activity, the heart beats about 70 times a minute.

◀ A doctor checks a patient's heartbeat to make sure her heart is working properly.

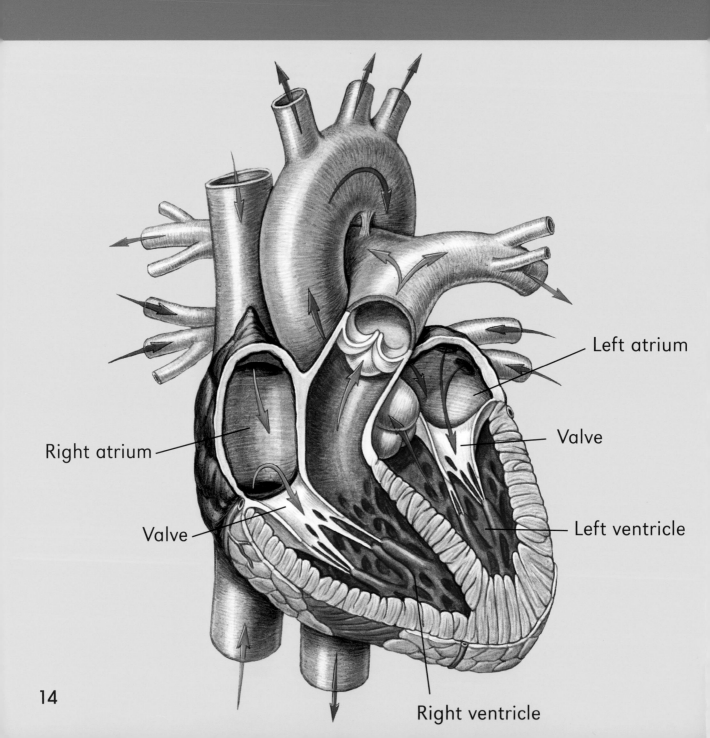

Left atrium

Valve

Left ventricle

Right atrium

Valve

Right ventricle

How the Heart Works

The heart has four chambers. The top two chambers are called atria. Blood flows through the atria before going to the lower chambers, or ventricles. When the heart squeezes, ventricles send blood out through arteries.

Blood flows between chambers through flaps called valves. Valves keep blood flowing in the right direction. Your heartbeat is the sound of the valves closing.

◄ The blue and red arrows show how blood travels through the heart.

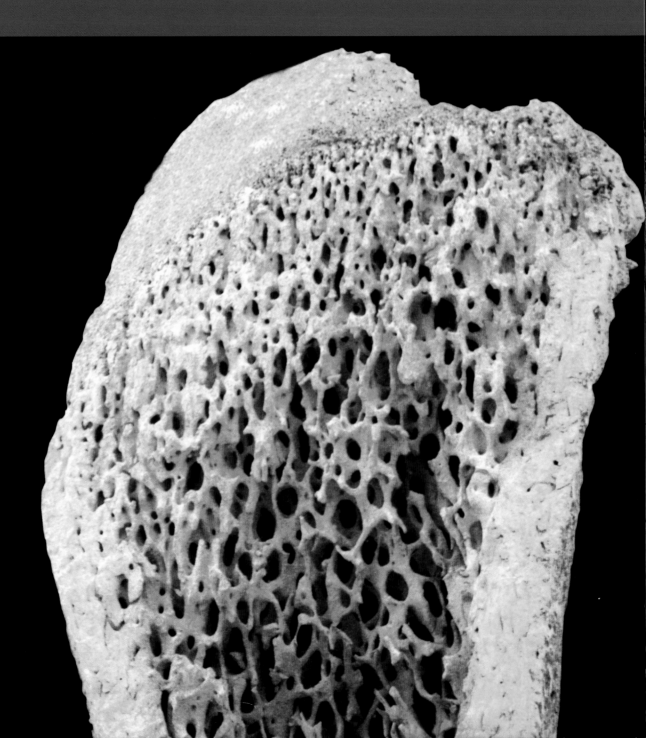

16

Calcium from Blood to Bones

Your bones, heart, muscles, and nerves all need calcium to work properly. Your blood circulates the calcium throughout your body. When you drink a glass of milk, the milk travels to your small intestine. Once there, your blood picks up the calcium from the milk.

Blood carries most of the calcium to your bones. Bones need calcium to stay strong, so they don't break when you fall. Your bones also store calcium. If you don't eat or drink enough calcium, your blood takes it from your bones.

◄ Calcium is stored inside bones.

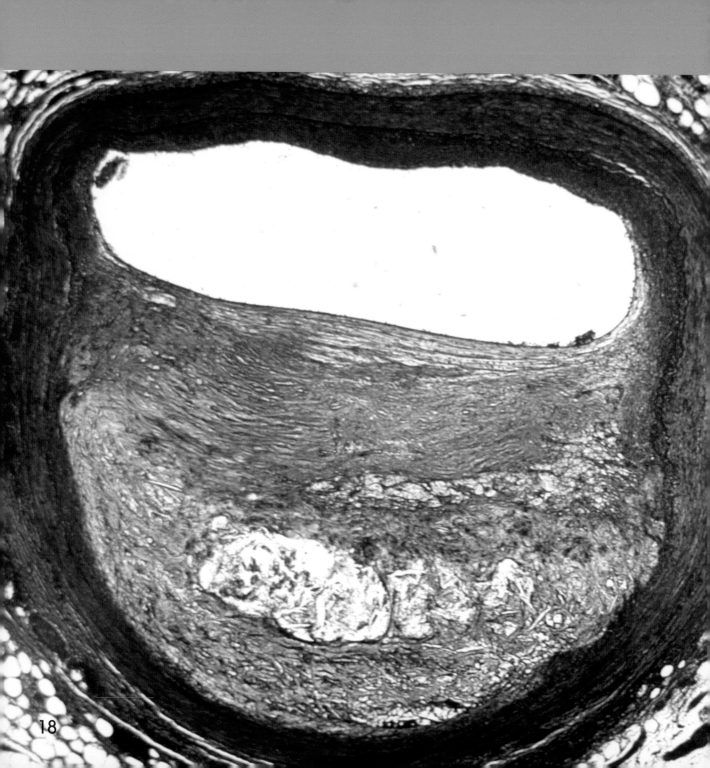

Circulatory Problems

Sometimes blood vessels harden or clog with fat. It's harder for blood to travel through plugged vessels. Imagine you are running through a tunnel that is filling up with dirt. You have to shimmy to get through. Just like blood squeezing past fat, you have a hard time getting to the other side. If blood vessels completely plug, no blood can flow through.

A heart attack happens when the heart does not get enough blood. Clogged arteries and blood **clots** can cause heart attacks. Blood clots stop blood from flowing back to the heart. Heart attacks can cause death.

◄ In clogged arteries, blood has to squeeze through tiny openings.

Keeping a Healthy Heart

Eating healthy foods and exercising helps the heart. Fruits and vegetables are good for your heart because they are low in fat and high in vitamins. Too much fat can clog blood vessels. Activities like running, swimming, and biking make the heart beat faster. The heart gets stronger when it works.

Smoking is hard on the heart. People who smoke are twice as likely to have a heart attack. You can protect your heart by never smoking. Keeping a healthy heart should keep you healthy for years to come.

◄ Activities like swimming are good for your heart.

Glossary

artery (AR-tuh-ree)—a blood vessel that carries blood away from the heart

blood vessel (BLUHD VESS-uhl)—a tube that carries blood through your body; veins, arteries, and capillaries are blood vessels.

capillary (KAP-uh-ler-ee)—a blood vessel that carries blood to the smallest parts of the body; capillaries connect to arteries and veins.

cell (SEL)—a tiny part of the body; cells make up body parts and blood.

clot (KLOT)—blood that has become thicker or more solid

hemoglobin (HEE-muh-gloh-bin)—a substance in red blood cells that carries oxygen and gives blood its red color

platelet (PLATE-lit)—a substance in blood that helps stop cuts from bleeding

vein (VAYN)—a blood vessel that carries blood back to the heart

Read More

Curry, Don L. *How Does Your Heart Work?*. Rookie Read-about Health. New York: Children's Press, 2003.

DeGezelle, Terri. *Your Heart.* Bridgestone Science Library. Mankato, Minn.: Bridgestone Books, 2002.

Internet Sites

FactHound offers a safe, fun way to find Internet sites related to this book. All of the sites on FactHound have been researched by our staff.

Here's how:

1. Visit *www.facthound.com*
2. Type in this special code **0736854088** for age-appropriate sites. Or enter a search word related to this book for a more general search.
3. Click on the **Fetch It** button.

FactHound will fetch the best sites for you!

Index